The Papers of
George Catlett Marshall

The Papers of
George Catlett Marshall

Volume 3

"THE RIGHT MAN FOR THE JOB"
DECEMBER 7, 1941 – MAY 31, 1943

Larry I. Bland, Editor

Sharon Ritenour Stevens, Associate Editor

THE JOHNS HOPKINS UNIVERSITY PRESS
Baltimore and London
1991

The Johns Hopkins University Press
701 West 40th Street
Baltimore, Maryland 21211
The Johns Hopkins Press Ltd., London

The paper used in this book meets the minimum requirements of
American National Standard for Information Sciences—Permanence
of Paper for Printed Library Materials, ANSI Z39.48-1984.

Library of Congress Cataloging in Publication Data

(Revised for volume 3)

Marshall, George C. (George Catlett), 1880-1959.
The papers of George Catlett Marshall.

Includes indexes.
Contents: v. 1. "The soldierly spirit," December 1880–June 1939.
v. 2. "We cannot delay," July 1, 1939–December 6, 1941.
v. 3. "The right man for the job," December 7, 1941–May 31, 1943.
1. Marshall, George C. (George Catlett), 1880-1959.
2. United States—History, Military—20th century—Sources.
3. Generals—United States—Correspondence.
4. United States. Army—Biography.

I. Bland, Larry I. II. Ritenour, Sharon R.   III. Title.
E745.M37 1981   973.918′092′4   81-47593
ISBN 0-8018-2552-0 (v. 1)
ISBN 0-8018-2553-9 (v. 2)
ISBN 0-8018-2967-4 (v. 3)

*The preparation and publication of this volume was made possible in
part by grants from the National Historical Publications and Records
Commission, an independent federal agency.*

Contents

Preface

THE MARSHALL PAPERS

The George C. Marshall Research Library is the repository for General Marshall's personal papers. Since 1956 this collection has been supplemented by contributions of documents by the general's friends, associates, and admirers and by the Marshall Foundation's program of copying relevant documents in other repositories, primarily the National Archives. The core of this volume was drawn from nearly fifty linear feet of material in the Pentagon Office subgroup of the Marshall papers. A detailed description of this and other series is given in John N. Jacob, *George C. Marshall Papers, 1932–1960: A Guide* (Lexington, Va.: George C. Marshall Foundation, 1987). Collateral collections are briefly described in Anita M. Weber, *Manuscript Collections of the George C. Marshall Library: A Guide* (Lexington, Va.: George C. Marshall Foundation, 1986).

This volume represents a selection from the Marshall material available to the editors. Of course, these documents do not indicate the complete scope of the army chief of staff's concerns. For example, key War Department personnel had offices near his and they frequently visited or talked on the telephone with Marshall. For a more comprehensive view of Marshall's activities, consult Forrest C. Pogue, *George C. Marshall,* 4 vols. (New York: Viking Press, 1963–87) and volumes in the series *United States Army in World War II.*

With few exceptions, these documents were written or dictated by General Marshall himself; occasionally he so substantially modified a staff-produced draft that the editors have considered it Marshall's. The texts of most documents published herein were taken from carbon copies in Marshall's files. On these the drafter's initials usually appear in the top right corner of the carbon copy and the typist's initials in the bottom left corner.

As the head of a large bureaucracy, Marshall signed numerous documents which he had not drafted. For example, many important staff-drafted radio messages from the War Department to field commanders were sent over the chief of staff's signature (rather than The Adjutant General's) to emphasize their importance. Scholars are often less concerned about who actually drafted a document than with who authorized or signed it. Thus there are numerous citations in the secondary literature to important documents emanating from Marshall's office and bearing his name that have not been included here. This volume does not seek to publish the papers of the Office of the Chief of Staff but only those created by the chief of staff himself. Regardless of their importance, staff-written documents are not usually included. Nevertheless, the chief of staff carefully oversaw the contents of documents produced for his signature. Colonel William T. Sexton, assistant secretary of the General Staff, informed Colonel Cyrus Q. Shelton of the Organization and Training Division (G-3): "When writing letters for General Marshall's signature, brevity should be the key note. The conversational style is always appealing to him, and all stereotyped expressions should be avoided, as well as all superlatives, except where obviously appropriate. His style is frank, warm, and polite regardless of the individual involved. Where a 'turndown' is involved, he is regretful. He dislikes such expressions as 'I am pleased to advise' and 'this will acknowledge receipt of.' He definitely does not like certain words which are used in typical letters written by the AGO such as 'therein,' 'thereupon,' and 'therefore.'" (Sexton Memorandum for Colonel Shelton, December 8, 1942, NA/RG 165 [OCS, 310].)

In this volume, the editors have reproduced 632 documents. Of these, 3 were not produced by Marshall but were included because the editors believed that they were relevant to the published edition. Most documents were dictated by Marshall to a secretary, usually Mona K. Nason; 5 documents were handwritten. In the annotation, the editors have cited an additional 139 documents by Marshall, 308 to him, and 209 other unpublished documents. Forty-six illustrations and eight maps have been reproduced.

ACKNOWLEDGMENTS

Clarence E. Wunderlin, Jr., assistant editor, 1982–87, was initially responsible for the selection of documents and annotation of the chapter "Sundays are Like Mondays."

Sharon Ritenour Stevens, associate editor, was responsible for chapters "The Pace of Modern War" and "Invincible Will To Win" as well as for the photographs, their captions, the list of illustrations, and portions of the chronology.

Joellen K. Bland keyed the volume into the editing terminal-typesetter, produced the galleys, and performed other essential technical duties.

Marshall Foundation archivist and librarian John N. Jacob and assistant archivist Anita M. Weber contributed essential archival services.

The members of the Marshall Papers Advisory Committee offered valuable advice on the entire volume, and they deserve special thanks for their work. The committee consisted of Gordon R. Beyer (Marshall Foundation president), Edward M. Coffman, (professor of military history, University of Wisconsin-Madison), Richardson Dougall (former deputy director, Historical Office, Department of State), William M. Franklin (former director, Historical Office, Department of State), Maurice Matloff (former chief historian, Center of Military History, Department of the Army), Forrest C. Pogue (General Marshall's authorized biographer), and Edwin A. Thompson (director, Records Declassification Division, National Archives and Records Administration).

The National Historical Publications and Records Commission and its staff have given the editors vital moral and financial support since the Marshall papers project was initiated in 1976. Without this support, the project very likely could not be done. Marshall Foundation fundraising efforts on behalf of the project were led by Gerald L. Nay, director of development.

The project has enjoyed close and beneficial relations with The Johns Hopkins University Press, and for that the editors would like to thank Barbara Lamb, managing editor, Henry Y. K. Tom, executive editor, and Robert J. Brugger, acquisitions editor.

Assistance in illustrating this volume was given by André Studio of Lexington, Virginia; Charlene N. Bickford of the First Federal Congress Project, George Washington University; William Cunliffe, director, Special Archives Division, National Archives and Records Administration; James E. Dedrick of the Lexington (Virginia) *News-Gazette;* Bill Kelley of Kelley Advertising Art; and Kathleen A. Struss of the Dwight D. Eisenhower Library.

Without the assistance of historians and archivists from many repositories, no work such as this would be possible. The editors would like to express their appreciation for the help they received from the following persons: Joseph J. Hovish of the American Legion Library; Holly MacKenzie of the *Asheville* (North Carolina) *Citizen-Times* Library; Dwight E. Strandberg of the Dwight D. Eisenhower Library; Robert Parks and Raymond Teichman of the Franklin D. Roosevelt Library; Charles Warren Ohrvall of the Harry S. Truman Library; Edward J. Boone, Jr., of the MacArthur Memorial; Donald L. Singer of the National Historical Publications and Records Commission; Richard J. Sommers and David A. Keough of the United States Army Military History Institute; Dawn L. Crupler of the United States Military Academy Library; Alice S. Creighton of the United States Naval Academy Library; Thelma J. Scott of the Waynesburg College Library; Robert B. Van Atta of Greensburg, Pennsylvania; George McJimsey of Iowa State University; and James J. Winn, Jr., of Baltimore, Maryland.

The editors also wish to thank the staffs of the Virginia Military Institute's Preston Library—especially Elizabeth S. Hostetter and Janet S. Holly—and of the Washington and Lee University Library.

The editors gratefully acknowledge the permission of the following publishers and institutions to reproduce materials: Yale University Library, for the numerous quotations from the diary of Henry L. Stimson; the Bettmann Archive; Time Inc.; and the *Washington Post.*

An aerial view of the Pentagon Building looking toward the District of Columbia, 1947. The south parking lot is in the extreme foreground, and the Potomac River, Memorial Bridge, and Lincoln Memorial are in view.

Guide to Editorial Policies

STYLE

Document texts and quotations in the annotation follow the writer's style, except as noted below. The editors' style generally conforms to that prescribed by *The Chicago Manual of Style,* 13th ed. (Chicago: University of Chicago Press, 1982).

TEXTUAL CHANGES AND INSERTIONS

Document Heading. The organization, sequence, and sometimes the content of the document heading have been supplied by the editors. This heading consists of between three and seven elements: addressee, date, originator, place of origin, message designation, security classification, and title.

The addressee for letters, telegrams, and radio messages is always in the form TO HARRY S. TRUMAN. Civil titles (i.e., Senator, Dr., The Honorable, Judge, etc.) are not included in the document heading. If the recipient was a married woman, Marshall usually used "Mrs." with her husband's name, if he knew it (e.g., Mrs. James J. Winn rather than Molly B. Winn). The editors have used the form Marshall indicated. For military personnel, including retired professionals, the rank used is that correct as of the date of the document. No distinction is made between permanent and temporary ranks in the annotation.

The addressee for memorandums is usually in the form MEMORANDUM FOR ___. The form of address Marshall used is followed, but abbreviations (e.g., A.C.S., Col., etc.) have been spelled out. If the memorandum is to an addressee's title only, that officer's last name is usually supplied in brackets or explained in a footnote (excepting the president and the secretary of war). A list of high-ranking War Department officials and theater commanders is printed in the Appendix.

Salutation and Complimentary Close. When present, these elements have been printed with the first and last lines respectively of the document text rather than on separate lines as they appear in the original. The capitalization and punctuation of the original have been retained.

Signature. Most documents in this volume have been reproduced from file (i.e., carbon) copies in the Marshall papers or in various War Department records. A name or initials at the end of a document published herein indicates that the editors have used the signed original as the source text.

Silent Corrections. In making silent corrections, the editors distinguished between documents physically produced by the author and those produced from dictation by a secretary. No silent changes have been introduced into author-produced documents. In documents typed by a secretary, the original capitalization and punctuation have been retained, but spelling errors have been silently corrected. Marshall sometimes made minor technical corrections to documents prior to having them sent. These changes are accepted as the final version of the source text. (See *Radio, Telegraph, and Cable Messages.*)

Brackets.   All information within brackets in this volume has been supplied by the editors. If the bracketed material is in italic type, it is to be read in place of the preceding word or letter (e.g., "fixed up for these four [*three*] divisions"). If the bracketed material is in roman type, it indicates additional rather than substitute information (e.g., "Wednesday afternoon [August 1] General Pershing").

Italics for Emphasis.   Except where used in brackets, italic type appears in the text of a document or in a quotation only if the emphasis was in the original—indicated on the source text by underlining.

Cross-references.   Citations to previous volumes in this series are usually given as: *Papers of GCM,* 1: 000. References to documents within this volume are in the form: (a) letters: Marshall to Embick, date, p. 000; (b) memorandums: Marshall Memorandum for the President, date, p. 000.

Security Classification.   The security classification is given in italic type beneath the sender-recipient line. War Department procedures regarding classification were not clarified and coordinated until 1944; consequently it is not uncommon to find copies of a document marked with different classifications in different files. Occasionally documents in the chief of staff's papers were not marked with a classification; if it is known from another source, the classification is indicated in brackets.

Radio, Telegraph, and Cable Messages.   For many messages it is impossible to establish the precise methods by which they were transmitted; the need for speed, the existence of transmission lines, atmospheric conditions, or simply the message center's convenience sometimes influenced the selection of a transmission medium. The term "Radio" is used to designate messages whether sent by radio, telegraph line, submarine cable, or some combination of these.

When such a message is addressed to an agency, office, official, or specific person for transmission to a designated addressee, the ultimate recipient is given (e.g., To LIEUTENANT GENERAL DWIGHT D. EISENHOWER rather than To THE ADJUTANT GENERAL). The sender's message number is included if known.

As prepared by the sender's office, radio messages usually included at the top as the address line certain instructions to the recipient's message center, e.g., "For General MacArthur's eyes alone." To inhibit cryptanalysis by the enemy, the transmitting agency usually buried these phrases within the transmitted text. Thus the location of address line will vary on different versions of the message. If the internal address on the source document is at the beginning, it is indented; if the editors have *moved* the internal address from the document text to the beginning, there is no paragraph indentation.

Depending on the version used as a source text, radio messages may be in standard form (i.e., upper- and lower-case letters with punctuation marks) or in all capitals with spelled-out punctuation. In the latter case, the editors have silently converted the text to standard form, including converting spelled-out numbers, dates, and names (e.g., B-17). The editors silently correct punctuation in radio messages.

DOCUMENT SOURCE CITATIONS

Source Line. At the end of each document and prior to the footnotes, the source of the document is listed in the following format: Repository/Collection (Main entry, Subentry). Several copies may exist of certain documents, and these may be found in different repositories or collections. The version used by the editors as the source text is the one cited. The abbreviations used in the source citations are listed in the Glossary.

Manuscript-type Notation. Holograph documents are designated by an "H" at the end of the document source line. Silent corrections have been made very rarely (e.g., the addition of an omitted period at the end of a sentence which itself ends at the edge or the bottom of a page on the original manuscript). Marshall documents not designated by "H" are presumed to have been produced by a clerk or secretary from dictation, notes, or a draft.

ANNOTATION

In the annotation the editors have attempted, insofar as possible, to explain all potentially obscure references, to provide cross-references to important related material, and to summarize the key parts of incoming or outgoing documents of relevance. The Marshall papers project is intended to provide a cohesive, intelligible story of Marshall in his own words, not to provide a detailed discussion of every facet of the general's life or to examine numerous questions not mentioned in Marshall documents.

In the annotation, the editors have sought to avoid using secondary sources, which would date the edition. An exception to this policy has been made for certain official military histories, particularly the indispensable series *United States Army in World War II* (Washington: GPO, 1947-).

Whenever appropriate and feasible, quotations from Marshall documents not selected for publication or from other primary sources have been used to annotate the published documents.

The editors have not cited individual uses of certain reference works: *Official National Guard Register; Army Directory: Reserve and National Guard Officers on Active Duty, July 31, 1941; Official Army Register; Army Directory; Cullum's Biographical Register of the Officers and Graduates of the U.S. Military Academy; The 1989 Register of Former Cadets of the Virginia Military Institute; Who's Who in America,* and Shelby L. Stanton, *Order of Battle: U.S. Army, World War II* (Novato, Calif.: Presidio Press, 1984).

Graduates of the two federal service academies and the Virginia Military Institute have been identified by school and year of graduation (e.g., V.M.I., 1901) the first time that person is cited in the Marshall papers volumes. Initial personal identifications include only the status, rank, or role at the time of the citation. Subsequent citations usually give only the changes since the previous citation. The indexes to the volumes will enable the reader to follow a particular individual's development or relationship to Marshall.

Illustrations

The following are the sources for the illustrations used in this volume.

frontispiece

General George C. Marshall during his visit to Fort Benning, Georgia, June 7–8, 1942. U.S. Army Signal Corps Photo 135958; GCMRL/Photographs (4088).

page xii

An aerial view of the Pentagon Building looking toward the District of Columbia, 1947. U.S. Army Signal Corps Photo 282473; GCMRL/Photographs (7167).

page 17

Document, Marshall to War Plans Division, December 12, 1941. NA/RG 165 (WPD, 4622).

following page 224

1. Marshall delivers a speech at the Reserve Officers' Association's National Council Dinner, January 9, 1942. U.S. Army Signal Corps Photo 128066; GCMRL/Photographs (2589).

2. General Marshall and Secretary of War Henry L. Stimson confer in the War Department, January 1942. U.S. Army Signal Corps Photo 128203; GCMRL/Photographs (1050).

3. Chiefs of the War Department confer, March 1942. U.S. Army Signal Corps Photo 130482; GCMRL/Photographs (3341).

4. Marshall visits Salisbury Plain during the London Conference, April 1942. GCMRL/Photographs (224).

5. Prime Minister Churchill and General Marshall during the trip to Salisbury Plain, April 1942. GCMRL/Photographs (225).

6. Field Marshal Sir John Dill and General Marshall visit Lee Mansion, April 28, 1942. Photo by Abbie Rowe—Courtesy National Park Service; GCMRL/Photographs (2892).

7. Sir John Dill and Marshall inspect a Parachute Infantry unit at Pope Field, Fort Bragg, North Carolina, May 1–2, 1942. U.S. Army Signal Corps Photo 134851; GCMRL/Photographs (1678).

8. Oveta Culp Hobby is sworn in as director of the Women's Army Auxiliary Corps by Major General Myron C. Cramer, May 16, 1942. Marshall and Secretary of War Henry L. Stimson witness the ceremony. U.S. Army Signal Corps Photo 133387; GCMRL/Photographs (358).

9. President Roosevelt and army and navy chiefs review the Memorial Day parade in Washington, D.C., on May 30, 1942. Joining the president are Field Marshal Sir John Dill, General Marshall, Captain John L. McCrea, and Admiral Ernest J. King. GCMRL/Photographs (1379).

10. President Roosevelt presents the Congressional Medal of Honor to Brigadier General James H. Doolittle, May 19, 1942. Witnessing the ceremony are Lieutenant General Henry H. Arnold, Mrs. Doolittle, and General Marshall. GCMRL/Photographs (6829).

11. General Marshall signs the Second Armored Division's guest book at Fort Benning, Georgia, June 7–8, 1942. Major General Willis D. Crittenberger is holding the book as Major General Lloyd R. Fredendall looks on. U.S. Army Photo; GCMRL/Photographs (6188).

12. General Marshall and his guests take part in a demonstration at Lawson Field, Fort Benning, Georgia, June 8, 1942. U.S. Army Signal Corps Photo 140238; GCMRL/Photographs (2988A).

13. Vice Admiral Lord Louis Mountbatten, Field Marshal Sir John Dill, General Marshall, and Major General Mark W. Clark tour Fort Bragg, North Carolina, June 9, 1942. U.S. Army Photo; GCMRL/Photographs (6198).

14. Prime Minister Churchill observes a demonstration at Fort Jackson, South Carolina, June 24, 1942. U.S. Army Signal Corps Photo 137584; GCMRL/Photographs (219).

15. Director Oveta Culp Hobby inspects barracks with Colonel Don C. Faith where Women's Army Auxiliary Corps women are new arrivals at the W.A.A.C. Training Center, Fort Des Moines, Iowa, July 20, 1942. GCMRL/Signal Corps Photographs (138812).

16. General George C. Marshall, June 1942. U.S. Army Signal Corps Photo 145960; GCMRL/Photographs (489).

17. General Marshall inspects troops of the Iceland Base Command, July 26, 1942. U.S. Army Photo; GCMRL/Photographs (339A).

18. General George C. Marshall appears on the cover of *Time,* October 19, 1942. Copyright © 1942 Time Inc. Reprinted by permission.

Chronology
December 2, 1941–May 31, 1943

The following is a list of the more important events of Marshall's life (in roman type) and of influence on his job (in italic type) during the period covered by this volume. All events involving General Marshall (GCM) took place in Washington, D.C., Fort Myer, Virginia, or the Pentagon Building unless otherwise noted. The editors have listed all known trips away from Washington. During the warmer months, Marshall spent some weekends at his house (Dodona Manor) in Leesburg, Virginia. Marshall's secretaries kept diaries of appointments, conferences, meetings, and trips, but these usually omit his office routine—i.e., his frequent meetings with the secretary of war and his personal staff and the visits of most members of the General Staff. (These diaries are in GCMRL/G. C. Marshall Papers [Pentagon Office, Engagement and Visitor Records].)

This chronology omits most of the numerous social and diplomatic luncheons, receptions, and dinners Marshall attended, but it includes all White House meetings and their main subjects, if known. Except during the major U.S.-U.K. conferences in Washington, the frequent meetings of three committees—the War Council, the Joint Chiefs of Staff, and the Combined Chiefs of Staff—are also excluded. The War Council (Secretary of War Henry L. Stimson and his advisers) usually met weekly on Monday morning until September 1942, when it shifted to Wednesday morning. Marshall was frequently absent; he attended only two meetings during the first five months of 1943. At the first Washington Conference [ARCADIA] in January 1942, United States and British leaders agreed to initiate meetings in Washington between the heads of the United States military services and representatives of the British Chiefs of Staff Committee: the Combined Chiefs of Staff (C.C.S.). The first such meeting was held on January 23, 1942. Prior to July 1942, meetings were generally held on Tuesdays at 2:30 or 3:00 P.M., although there were numerous exceptions; in July they were switched to Thursdays and then in August to Fridays. Faced with the necessity of presenting a reasonably united front to the British, the United States service heads replaced the old Joint Board with the Joint Chiefs of Staff (J.C.S.) committee, which held its first meeting on February 9, 1942. From the first, Marshall insisted that the Army Air Forces be represented at the meetings, and during the summer of 1942 he convinced the president to balance the two army votes with another navy vote by including Admiral William D. Leahy (chief of staff to the commander in chief), who was chairman of the committee. Joint Chiefs of Staff meetings were usually held on Mondays at 2:00 or 2:30 P.M. during the first four months, shifting to Tuesday afternoons in June 1942. Beginning in September 1942 these meetings were frequently preceded by a luncheon.

December 1941

2   *Japanese Cabinet reaffirms decision to attack Pearl Harbor (force had sailed November 26).*

7   *Pearl Harbor Naval Base and nearby army bases attacked by Japanese carrier aircraft beginning at 7:50 A.M. local time.* White House meeting, about 2:00 P.M.

8   Remarks to editors of black newspapers, 10:30 A.M. Attends president's speech to Congress. Special Joint Board meeting, 2:45 P.M.

10 White House meeting regarding Martinique and convoy to Philippines. *Japanese troops land in northwest Luzon. British troops break siege of Tobruk.*

11 *Germany and Italy declare war on U.S. and U.S. on them.*

16 White House meeting regarding aircraft and materiel for the Far East.

18 *First War Powers Act passed giving the president power to reorganize executive agencies.* White House meeting on ARCADIA Conference arrangements and agenda.

21 *Massive Japanese landings in Philippines.* White House meeting on strategic concerns at ARCADIA Conference.

22 *First U.S. troops arrive in Australia. Churchill and advisers arrive in Washington.*

23 *Wake Island surrenders. MacArthur decides to evacuate Luzon for a stand in Bataan.* ARCADIA Conference begins with White House plenary session, 4:45 P.M.

24 U.S.–U.K. military leaders meeting, 10:30 A.M.

25 U.S.–U.K. military leaders meeting, 4:00 P.M. White House meeting with president and advisers, 5:30 P.M.

26 U.S.–U.K. military leaders meeting, 3:00 P.M. Conference plenary session, White House, 4:30 P.M.

27 Meeting with prime minister, White House, morning. Meeting with president, 10:00 A.M. U.S.–U.K. military leaders meeting, 3:00 P.M.

28 Meeting with president and military advisers, 11:45 A.M.

29 Meeting with Hopkins and Stimson, 2:30 P.M. U.S.–U.K. military leaders meeting, 4:00 P.M.

30 U.S.–U.K. military leaders meeting, 3:00 P.M.

31 U.S.–U.K. military leaders meeting, 2:00 P.M.

January 1942

1   Conference plenary session, White House, 6:00 P.M. *Declaration by United Nations signed by U.S., U.K., U.S.S.R., China, 10:00 P.M. (other nations sign later).*

3   Standing Liaison Committee meeting, noon. *A.B.D.A. Command under Wavell announced.*

4   Conference plenary session, White House, 5:30 P.M.

5   Travels to Miami with Churchill (returns same day).

6   *Stationing of U.S. troops in Britain announced.*

9   Informal speech at Reserve Officers' Association dinner.

10   U.S.–U.K. military leaders meeting, 3:00 P.M.

11   U.S.–U.K. military leaders meeting, 4:00 P.M. White House meeting with president, 5:30 P.M.

12   U.S.–U.K. military leaders meeting, 4:00 P.M. Conference plenary session, White House, 5:30 P.M.

13   U.S.–U.K. military leaders meeting, 4:00 P.M. *Arnold-Portal Agreement signed allocating U.S.-produced aircraft.*

14   *U-boats begin sinkings along U.S. East Coast.* U.S.–U.K. military leaders meeting, 3:00 P.M. Final ARCADIA Conference plenary session, White House, 5:30 P.M.

19   Testifies before Roberts Commission concerning his actions on the morning of December 7, 1941 (committee report issued 24th). White House meeting, 2:15 P.M.

21   Joint Board meeting, 11:15 A.M.

23   First C.C.S. meeting, 3:00 P.M.

26   *Japanese capture Rabaul. Bataan defenders fall back to final defense line. First contingent of U.S. forces arrives in Northern Ireland.*

28   Joint Board meeting, 11:30 A.M. White House conference with navy and British, 2:00 P.M.

February 1942

6   White House lunch with president, 1:00 P.M. Departs for West Point, 3:20 P.M. (returns 7th, 4:45 P.M.).

7   *War Shipping Administration established.*

9   White House meetings concerning Philippines, 10:30 A.M., 2:30 P.M..

10   Standing Liaison Committee meeting, 10:00 A.M.

11   White House conference regarding the Philippines and reinforcements for the Far East, 3:00 P.M.

15   *Singapore surrenders to Japanese.*

19   White House conference on strategic shipping, noon. *Executive Order 9066 permits War Department to establish military areas in U.S. and to exclude or restrict persons from them (the basis for Japanese-American removals).*

20 Joint Board meeting, 11:30 A.M.

22 *MacArthur ordered to leave the Philippines.*

24 White House meeting with president regarding MacArthur's refusal to leave Philippines.

26 *Army Specialist Corps established (abolished November 4).*

28 Joint Board meeting, 11:30 A.M.

March 1942

5 White House conference regarding general war strategy, 2:00 P.M.

7 White House conference regarding general war strategy, noon.

9 *Official date of War Department reorganization.*

12 *MacArthur and party depart for Australia (arrives 17th).*

20 Standing Liaison Committee meeting, 11:00 A.M.

21 *Voluntary evacuation of Japanese-Americans from West Coast begins (compulsory evacuation begins 31st).*

23 *War Plans Division renamed Operations Division.*

25 *Medal of Honor for MacArthur announced (citation written by GCM).* White House luncheon, 1:00 P.M.

26 *Admiral Ernest J. King becomes chief of naval operations.*

28 Departs for Richmond, Va., 10:45 A.M. (returns 29th).

30 Addresses opening session of the Inter-American Defense Board, 11:00 A.M. *Pacific Theater divided into Pacific Ocean Areas (navy) and Southwest Pacific Area (MacArthur). Pacific War Council established.*

April 1942

1 White House meeting, 2:30 P.M.; president approves BOLERO-ROUNDUP plans.

4 Departs for London Conference, 7:00 A.M. (trip delayed in Bermuda by engine trouble until 7th).

8 Arrives in London; meets with Churchill.

9 *Bataan forces surrender.* Formal presentation to British of plans for Western European operations.

13 British Chiefs of Staff give qualified endorsement to U.S. strategy in Europe (Churchill accepts 14th).

16 Reviews British troops on Salisbury Plain.

17 Final meeting with Churchill.

18 Reviews U.S. Army forces in Northern Ireland. *Army newspaper* Stars and Stripes *resumes publication with statement by GCM. James H. Doolittle leads B-25 raid on Japan. War Manpower Commission established.*

19 Returns from London Conference, about 4:00 P.M.

20   White House luncheon, 1:00 P.M.

21   Off-the-record press conference, 10:30 A.M.

22   Discusses London trip with members of Senate and House Appropriations and Military Affairs committees, 10:00 A.M. (similar talk with another group of senators 23d).

24   Local flight with Arnold, 11:00 A.M. In-flight inspection of air-to-surface radar with Stimson.

25   Departs for Edward R. Stettinius home in Albemarle County, Va., 11:00 A.M. (returns 26th).

29   *Japanese troops cut Burma Road at Lashio. British decide to withdraw from Burma.*

30   Departs with Sir John Dill to inspect southern army posts, 7:30 A.M. (returns May 2, about 2:15 P.M.).

May 1942

6   *Corregidor surrenders—end of formal resistance in the Philippines; organized resistance ends June 9.*

7   White House meeting regarding Australian aid requests, 10:45 A.M.

7–8   *Battle of the Coral Sea.*

15   Attends signing ceremony for Women's Army Auxiliary Corps bill, White House, 3:30 P.M.

16   Attends swearing in of Oveta Culp Hobby as WAAC director.

17   Departs for Hollins College, Va., with Mrs. GCM, 8:15 A.M. She delivers address at college's centenary celebration. Returns to Washington, evening.

20   White House meeting, 2:00 P.M.

22   Departs on trip to inspect Western Defense Command, 2:00 P.M. (returns 26th, 3:15 P.M.).

27   White House meeting, 2:00 P.M.

28   Departs for West Point, 2:00 P.M.

29   Delivers commencement address at U.S.M.A., 2:00 P.M. Arrives in Washington, 7:00 P.M.

30   White House conference with Roosevelt and Soviet Foreign Minister Molotov regarding Second Front, 11:00 A.M. Reviews parade with the president, 4:00 P.M.

June 1942

4–6   *Battle of Midway.*

7   Departs with Mountbatten and Dill to inspect southern army posts, 3:00 P.M. At Fort Benning, Ga.

8   At Fort Benning and Camp Gordon, Ga., Fort Jackson, S.C.

9   At Fort Bragg, N.C. Returns to Washington, noon. White House luncheon, 1:00 P.M.

11 White House meeting, 2:15 P.M.

12 White House luncheon, 1:00 P.M.

13 *Office of the Coordinator of Information becomes the Office of Strategic Services (O.S.S.) under J.C.S. control. Office of War Information established.* Departs for Leesburg, 12:15 P.M. (returns 14th).

15 Speaks to Women's Interest Section, Bureau of Public Relations, 10:00 A.M.

16 Informal talk to Leesburg Junior Board of Trade, 7:30 P.M.

17 White House meeting regarding North African invasion versus cross-Channel, 2:00 P.M.

19–25 Second Washington Conference.

19 C.C.S. meeting, 12:30 P.M.

20 C.C.S. meeting, 11:00 A.M.

21 Conference plenary sessions, White House, afternoon and 9:30 P.M.

23 Conference plenary session, White House, 2:40 P.M. Departs for Fort Jackson, S.C., with Churchill's party (returns 24th).

25 C.C.S. meeting, 9:30 A.M.

26 Departs for Leesburg, about noon (returns 28th).

July 1942

7 Off-the-record press conference, 11:30 A.M.

8 Departs with Arnold for Wright Field, Ohio, 3:30 P.M.

9 Travels to Fort Knox, Ky. Returns to Washington, 8:20 P.M.

11 Travels to Leesburg (returns 12th).

15 White House meeting regarding GYMNAST and BOLERO, 10:00 A.M.

16 White House meeting, about 11:00 A.M. Departs for London Conference, noon.

18–19 Confers with Eisenhower and staff in London.

20–22 Meetings in London with British Chiefs of Staff.

21 *President announces that Admiral Leahy is his personal chief of staff.*

24–25 Meetings in London with British Chiefs of Staff. Departs for Iceland.

26 Inspects troops in Iceland (returns to Washington 27th, 3:00 P.M.).

28 White House meeting regarding London trip, noon.

29 White House luncheon, 1:00 P.M.

30 Off-the-record press conference, 11:00 A.M.

31 Travels to Leesburg (returns August 2).

August 1942

7 White House luncheon with President and Mrs. Roosevelt, 1:00 P.M. *U.S. Marines land on Tulagi and Guadalcanal in the Solomon Islands.*

15 *Germans launch offensive designed to capture Stalingrad (halted by September 23).* Travels to Leesburg (returns 16th).

19   *U.S. Army Rangers participate in Dieppe Raid.*
22   Travels to Leesburg (returns 23d).
25   Remarks to Joint Brazil–U.S. Defense Commission, 12:45 P.M., for broadcast to Brazil.
28   White House meetings regarding C.C.S. deadlock on TORCH tactics, 1:00 and 2:00 P.M.
29   Departs for Leesburg, 11:00 A.M. (returns 30th).
30   *Adak Island in the Aleutians occupied by U.S. forces.* White House dinner, 7:15 P.M.
31   Off-the-record press conference, 2:30 P.M.

September 1942

1   White House meeting regarding TORCH, 4:45 P.M.
5   Travels to Leesburg (returns 6th).
12   Travels to Leesburg (returns 13th).
15   *First U.S. troops arrive in New Guinea.*
16   Meets with House Military Affairs Committee, 10:00 A.M.
17   Meets with Senate Committee on Military Affairs, 10:00 A.M.
19   Travels to Leesburg (returns 20th).
22   Testifies before Senate Committee on Military Affairs regarding transferring construction responsibilities to Corps of Engineers.
26   Departs for Leesburg, about 9:45 A.M. (returns 27th).
28   Special C.C.S. meeting with Mark W. Clark, 2:30 P.M.
29   Attends Irving Berlin's production "This Is the Army," 8:00 P.M.

October 1942

2   White House meeting regarding manpower, noon.
3   Departs for Fort Bragg, N.C., about 11:00 A.M. (returns 4th).
5   White House meeting regarding manpower, 10:30 A.M.
9   Meets with Pacific War Council, noon.
10   Off-the-record press conference, 11:15 A.M.
13   *First U.S. Army troops land on Guadalcanal.*
14   Testifies most of morning before House and Senate military committees in support of 18- and 19-year-olds draft bill.
22   Views "Prelude to War," first of Frank Capra's "Why We Fight" films, 1:30 P.M.
23   *British launch attack at El Alamein. TORCH convoy sails from Hampton Roads. Admiral Darlan arrives in Morocco.* White House conference regarding steel priorities and shipping, 11:30 A.M.
24   Departs for Richmond, Va., for VMI football game, 12:30 P.M.
29   *Alaska Military Highway opens.*
30   Off-the-record press conference, 11:45 A.M.

November 1942

4   *Decisive British break-through at battle of El Alamein.*

8   *TORCH landings near Casablanca, Oran, Algiers. Vichy France breaks relations with U.S.*

9   *Germans begin ferrying troops to Tunisia by air.* White House conference regarding TORCH, 2:30 P.M.

10   *Admiral Darlan issues cease-fire order to French troops in North Africa (fighting ends 11th).* Departs for New York City, 1:00 P.M., to speak at Academy of Political Science dinner (returns 11th, 7:15 A.M.).

11   *German troops occupy previously unoccupied areas of France.*

12   American Legion National Commander's dinner honors GCM.

13   *Bill to draft 18- and 19-year-olds signed.* Departs for West Point with Dill, 3:15 P.M. (returns 14th, about 7:00 P.M.).

15   Offices of secretary of war and chief of staff moved to the Pentagon Building. Off-the-record press conference regarding the Darlan affair.

18   Meets with members of the Senate and House military committees, 10:30 A.M.

19   *Soviet army launches winter offensive at Stalingrad (German Sixth Army surrounded by 22d).*

20   Departs late afternoon with Arnold for duck hunting with Glenn Martin near Baltimore, Md. (returns 21st).

25   White House conference regarding war production, 2:30 P.M.

30   *Germans launch four-day counterattack that stops Allied drive on Bizerte-Tunis, leading to stalemate during the winter.*

December 1942

4   Departs for New York City, late afternoon, to speak at National Association of Manufacturers convention (returns 5th).

5   Hunting with Arnold near Manassas, Va. (returns 6th).

8   Civilian-military manpower luncheon and conference, 12:30 P.M.

10   White House meeting regarding manpower, 2:00 P.M.

19   Hunting with Arnold (returns 20th).

24   White House luncheon, 1:00 P.M. *Admiral Darlan assassinated in Algiers (succeeded as high commissioner by Giraud on 27th).*

28   White House conference regarding shipping, 10:00 A.M.

January 1943

4   Off-the-record press conference, 2:30 P.M.

7   White House meeting regarding strategy proposals at Casablanca Conference, 3:00 P.M.

9   Departs for Casablanca Conference via Puerto Rico, Brazil, Gambia; arrives Casablanca 13th.

14–24 Casablanca Conference

14 C.C.S meeting, 10:30 A.M. and 2:30 P.M. Dinner meeting with Churchill, Roosevelt, and C.C.S., 8:00 P.M.

15 J.C.S. meeting with the president, 10:00 A.M. C.C.S. meeting, 2:30 P.M. Dinner meeting with Churchill, Roosevelt, and C.C.S., 5:30 P.M.

16 C.C.S. meeting, 10:30 A.M. J.C.S. meeting with the president, 5:00 P.M.

17 C.C.S. meeting, 10:30 A.M.

18 C.C.S. meeting, 10:30 A.M. C.C.S. meeting with Churchill and Roosevelt, 5:00 P.M.

19 C.C.S. meeting, 10:00 A.M. and 4:00 P.M. (General Giraud attends part of this meeting).

20 C.C.S. meeting, 10:00 A.M. and 2:30 P.M.

21 C.C.S. meeting, 10:00 A.M.

22 C.C.S. meeting, 10:15 A.M. and 2:30 P.M.

23 C.C.S. meeting, 10:00 A.M. C.C.S. meeting with Churchill and Roosevelt, 5:30 P.M. C.C.S. meeting, 9:30 P.M.

24 Travels to Algiers to visit Eisenhower.

26 Returns to Casablanca. Departs for Washington (arrives 29th about 6:00 P.M.).

30 Off-the-record press conference, 2:00 P.M.

February 1943

2 *Stalingrad battle ends with German Sixth Army surrender.*

10 Meets with members of Senate and House military committees regarding manpower legislation, 10:30 A.M.

13 Informal talk to American Society of Newspaper Editors convention, 9:30 A.M. White House meeting, noon.

14 *German attack on U.S. Second Corps in Tunisia begins.*

20 *U.S. troops pushed out of Kasserine Pass.* White House meeting with Mme Chiang Kai-shek, 4:00 P.M.

22 *Germans begin withdrawing in southern Tunisia (operation completed 24th).*

26 Meets with Pacific War Council, noon.

March 1943

2–5 *Battle of the Bismarck Sea.*

3 Leaves office early with a cold; remains home through 6th.

7 Departs with Mrs. GCM for Miami Beach, Fla., for vacation (returns 14th, afternoon).

12–28 Pacific Military Conference.

21 Special J.C.S. meeting, 11:00 A.M.

22 Departs afternoon for inspection trip to the South with Eden and Dill (returns 24th).

23 Arrives at Fort Benning, Ga., in the evening.

24 Departs from Fort Benning, noon; arrives at Fort Bragg, N.C., in the afternoon. Returns to Washington by evening.

26 White House meeting regarding aircraft, 11:30 A.M.

28 Special J.C.S. meeting, 11:00 A.M.

30 White House meeting regarding a commission for Fiorello La Guardia, 10:45 A.M.

April 1943

5 Departs with Somervell for Erie, Pa., about 8:00 A.M. (returns 2:45 P.M.).

6 Informal address at the Military Order of the World War's Army Day luncheon, 12:30 P.M.

9 Special J.C.S. meeting, 2:30 P.M.

10 Departs for Leesburg, about 9:15 A.M. (returns in the afternoon).

18 *Admiral Isoroku Yamamoto killed in U.S. air attack when his travel plans are disclosed by cryptanalysis.*

23 Departs for inspection trip to Camp Pickett, Va., and Asheville, N.C. (returns 25th, about 6:00 P.M.).

24 Visits wounded soldiers at Moore General Hospital, Asheville, N.C.

29 Special J.C.S. meeting to hear Eaker's report on the Combined Bomber Offensive, 2:00 P.M. White House meeting, 3:30 P.M.

30 Meeting with Arnold, Stilwell, and Chennault, 10:30 A.M. White House meeting, 11:30 A.M.

May 1943

— *"Black May" for German U-boats as tide turns in favor of Allies in North Atlantic.*

3 *Frank M. Andrews, commander of U.S. Forces, European Theater of Operations, killed in Iceland air crash.*

7 *Allied forces occupy Tunis and Bizerte.* Conferences with Devers prior to his departing to replace Andrews.

8 Special J.C.S. meeting, 10:00 A.M.

9 *German forces on U.S. Second Corps front in Tunisia surrender.* White House meeting regarding TRIDENT Conference, 2:30 P.M.

10 Testifies before Senate Foreign Relations Committee, 10:00 A.M. Special J.C.S. meeting regarding TRIDENT Conference, 2:00 P.M.

11 *U.S. 7th Division lands on Attu, Aleutian Islands (island declared secure 30th).* Meeting in Leahy's White House office, 6:00 P.M., in preparation for Churchill's arrival.

12–25   TRIDENT Conference, Washington, D.C.

12   J.C.S. meeting, 11:30 A.M. White House meeting, 2:30 P.M. *General von Arnim formally surrenders all remaining Axis forces in Tunisia (fighting ends 13th).*

13   J.C.S. meeting, 10:15 A.M. C.C.S. meeting, 10:30 A.M.

14   J.C.S. meeting, 9:30 A.M. C.C.S. meeting, 10:30 A.M. Conference plenary session, White House, 2:00 P.M.

15   J.C.S. meeting, 9:30 A.M. C.C.S. meeting, 10:30 A.M. Departs with British Chiefs of Staff for Williamsburg, Va., afternoon.

16   Returns to Washington, about 12:45 P.M. Flies to Hagerstown, Md., then motors to "Shangri-la" camp for conference with Roosevelt and Churchill. Returns to Washington by midnight.

17   J.C.S. meeting, 9:30 A.M. C.C.S. meeting, 10:30 A.M. Conference plenary session, White House, 3:30 P.M.

18   J.C.S. meeting, 9:30 A.M. C.C.S. meeting, 10:30 A.M.

19   J.C.S. meeting, 9:30 A.M. C.C.S. meeting, 10:30 A.M. Conference plenary session, White House, 5:00 P.M.

20   J.C.S. meeting, 9:30 A.M. Meeting at White House with Churchill, 10:30 A.M. C.C.S. meeting, 11:30 A.M. Conference plenary session, White House, 3:30 P.M. British Chiefs of Staff dinner for U.S. Chiefs of Staff, 8:15 P.M.

21   J.C.S. meeting, 9:30 A.M. C.C.S. meeting, 10:30 A.M. Conference plenary session, White House, 5:00 P.M.

22   J.C.S. meeting, 9:30 A.M. C.C.S. meeting, 10:30 A.M.

23   J.C.S. meeting, 11:00 A.M. C.C.S. meeting, 2:00 P.M.

24   J.C.S. meeting, 9:30 A.M. C.C.S. meeting, 10:30 A.M. Conference plenary session, White House, 4:45 P.M.

25   C.C.S. meeting, 10:30 A.M. Conference plenary session, White House, 11:30 A.M. White House luncheon, 1:00 P.M.

26   Departs with Churchill for Algiers Conference, 8:30 A.M. (returns June 7).

The Sterner Realities

December 7, 1941–February 28, 1942

It is now only a few hours since this nation was attacked by one of the great armed forces of the world. Great as our efforts in the interest of national defense have been during the year which now draws to a close, events of the past day have brought to us the sterner realities of actual war.

—Address to Conference of Negro Newspaper Editors
December 8, 1941

GCMRL/G. C. Marshall Papers (Pentagon Office, Speeches)